Copyright

DISCLAIMER

This is an unofficial summary of the original book, *This is Your Brain on Food: An Indispensable Guide to the Surprising Food that Fight Depression, Anxiety, PTSD, OCD, ADHD, and more*, by Uma Naidoo, MD. It is written to capture the key points of the book and to help the reader understand the main gist of the book in much fewer words. It features cover questions and discussion questions which makes it serve as an effective study material.

Table of Contents

Background Information about Uma Naidoo

Uma Naidoo, MD is a nutritional psychiatrist and is often internationally regarded as the pioneer of the field. She trained at the Harvard Longwood Psychiatry Residency Program. She is also certified by the Cambridge School of Culinary Art as a Professional Chef. She currently serves as the director of nutritional and lifestyle psychiatry at the Massachusetts General Hospital.

Summary Overview of *This is Your Brain on Food: An Indispensable Guide to the Surprising Foods that Fight Depression, Anxiety, PTSD, OCD, ADHD, and More*

This is Your Brain on Food by Uma Naidoo, MD presents a detailed examination of the connection between nutrition and psychiatry – the gut and the brain. For Naidoo, the conventional approach of psychiatrists which entails the separation of brain health from nutrition is largely ineffective. She argues that there is a mutual relationship between nutrition (the food we eat) and mental health. This owes to the biological connection between the gut and the brain – the chemicals produced in the brain influence the gut and vice versa. Hence, for Naidoo, to effectively care for the brain, proper nutrition is indispensable.

In the book, Naidoo presents how mental issues like Anxiety, ADHD, PTSD, Bipolar Disorder, etc. are caused by nutrition deficiencies and how they can be cured or managed with the right diets. The book also features how specific diets, fruits, and spices that can be used to promote general mental health.

Introduction

For Uma Naidoo, even though there appears to be no natural correlation between Psychiatry and Nutrition, the case may be unlikely so. Of course, it is quite common to see psychiatrists prescribe drugs to their patients or refer them to some other types of therapy, yet it is unlikely to see any Psychiatrist offer guidance on foods that can help the patients address their challenges. In the same vein, while it is of common place to think about the impact of the foods we eat on our hearts, waistlines, and even our environments, it is generally rare to think about how the food we eat influence on our brains.

For Uma Naidoo, there is a mutual link between mental health and nutrition. She argues that poor diet often culminates in mental health issues. Just similarly, mental health issues also tend to result in poor feeding habits. Given this, she concludes that until nutritional problems are addressed effectively, no amount of medication will be able to provide lasting solutions to the myriads of mental issues in our societies.

To ensure general mental health, Uma Naidoo stresses the importance of addressing the mutual relationship between nutrition and mental health on individual levels – not only in those who are diagnosed with mental illnesses, but also in those who aren't. Irrespective of whether or not anyone has had issues with anxiety, depression etc., she argues that everyone has felt sad, nervous, experienced some form of trauma, obsession, and etc. Besides this, everyone wants to keep their memory and attention sharp, and to live normal healthy lives. Hence, she aims to show practical ways of achieving total mental health through diet.

Being a psychiatrist, a nutritionist, and a trained chef, Naidoo narrates how people have quite naturally often assumed that she started cooking before she became a psychiatrist. However, it turns out that she had only learnt to cook after she had already become a doctor. Having grown up among mother, grandmothers, aunts who were great cooks, she really didn't need to cook much while growing up. When she moved to Boston to train as a psychiatrist, she became separated from the delicious food and love she regularly enjoyed. This compelled her to start cooking. She began practicing all the recipes she had learnt, and soon mastered the art of cooking. She remained passionate about cooking, even when she began practicing as a psychiatrist. She enrolled in the Cambridge School of Culinary Arts, pledging her commitment to psychiatry and nutrition. The exposure to these two disciplines drew her closer to the nutritional value of food.

After graduating from culinary school, Naidoo also completed a program in Nutritional Science. Her knowledge of nutrition and culinary techniques influenced her practice of psychiatry and has, in her words, been the blueprint for her works and the founding of the *Nutrition and Lifestyle Psychiatry Program* at Massachusetts General Hospital.

Naidoo's education in Nutrition and Psychiatry was even more enhanced when she had a firsthand experience – she was diagnosed with cancer. However, this helped her apply her nutritional skills on her body and also helped her realize how a healthy lifestyle techniques was key to health. The lifestyle aspects are important just as healthy nutrition is to healing. Her experiences have thus inspired this book, with the hope of introducing the reader to Nutritional Psychiatry and to educate them on how to keep their body and brain healthy.

Chapter 1: The Gut-Brain Romance

In this chapter, Uma Naidoo carries out an examination into the history of mental illness and how the society responded to them. Up till around the 17th and 18th century, mentally ill people were housed in prisons. This was because their conditions were considered a sinful state. However, with the spread of civilization, this changed and they were moved from prisons to hospitals. But it turned out that, the more man paid attention to the particular realities of mental illnesses, somehow, we ceased to notice that the rest of the body was equally involved and affected. She argues that this hasn't always been the case

Naidoo makes reference to the historian, E.N Miller, who pointed out that 18th and 19th century doctors were aware of the direct connection of the body systems. This awareness, according to Miller, is why they spoke of the "nervous sympathy" among our body's different organs. However, as medicine became more specialized, doctors changed this perspective. They lost track of the big picture by only focusing on single organs to determine what is wrong or what needed to be treated. They failed to see that organs that are separate in the body could affect one another.

Another thing that compounded this problem was the fact that physicians, anatomists, surgeons, physiologists, psychologists, etc. got into an unhealthy competition one another instead of working collaboratively. This attitude has prevailed till date. It is as a result of this that many people have become ignorant of the fact that the root of mental illnesses isn't all in the brain. Rather, it can indicate that the connections with the brain have gone faulty.

Little changes in certain parts of the body can affect the brain too. The brain and the gut is a profound example here. Hippocrates, the father of modern medicine, spoke of this, centuries ago, when he warned that "bad digestion is the root of all evil." This reality of this is beginning to get more evident as more recent researches now dwell more on the topic of the gut-brain connection and the field of nutritional psychiatry.

Naidoo proves the natural connection between the brain and the gut through a simple analysis. She expresses that, before the eventual birth of a child (before the gut, brain and limbs all showed forth), they were all one – they came from the same fertilized egg (the zygote). After none months, this develops to show forth all the organs in one's body. This shows that, before the gut and the brain became distinct and separated, they were one. In line with this, the central nervous system which contains the brain and spinal cords is formed by ***Neural Crest cells***, which migrate throughout a developing embryo and forming the ***enteric nervous system***.

The gut contains the enteric nervous system which has the largest collection of nerve cells in the body – between 100 to 500 million neurons. This is why it is called the second brain. It also explains why the gut and the brain influence each other intricately, even though they appear distant. The ***Vagus Nerve*** which originates in the brain stem and extends to the gut is responsible for connecting the gut to the central nervous system. It plays an important role in food digestion but has the primary function of ensuring that nerve signals can travel between the gut and the brain, helping them to share information. This way, signals are shared between the gut and the brain, making them "lifelong partners."

Naidoo notes that, activities within the body – between the gut and the brain (through the vagus nerve) often takes place by chemicals. This is, for instance, demonstrated when one takes or swallow a pill. The pill finds its way into the gut which breaks it down. The chemicals thus travels from the gut to the brain through the blood stream, exerting the expected effect (i.e. kill pain).

Similarly, communication takes place when the chemicals produced by the gut are sent to the brain, and when those produced by the brain gets to the guts. The chemicals produced by the brain come from the primary part of the nervous system supported by the endocrine system, autonomic nervous system (ANS), HPA axis, and the central nervous system.

The ***central nervous system*** produces chemicals like dopamine, serotonin, etc. which are important for mood regulation, processing thoughts and emotions. Serotonin deficiency is responsible for depression and anxiety. Serotonin plays a key role in regulating the gut and brain communication. However, more than 90 percent of its receptors are found in the gut.

The ***autonomic nervous system*** (ANS), on the other hand, is in charge of a broad range of involuntary functions like the beating of the heart, breathing, food digestion, etc. It is also responsible for the "fight or flight" response (when the body is under duress or in danger. The gut plays a key role in the "fight or flight" response through the regulation of the hormone, adrenaline, and noradrenaline.

The ***HPA Axis*** produces hormones that stimulate the release of cortisol which equips the body to handle stress, supplying it with energy to deal with difficult situations. Once the difficult situation has been dealt with, it returns to normal. It helps the body respond to stress effectively.

These chemicals ensure that the gut-brain communication goes smoothly. However, in the case of a chemical imbalance or excessiveness or underproduction of these chemicals, this communication can be thrown into disarray, resulting in poor mood, concentration, immunity, etc. These chaos give rise to psychiatric symptoms like anxiety, depression, and loss of libido, schizophrenia, and bipolar disorder. While good pharmaceuticals play important roles in altering these chemicals and restoring balance, the food one eats can be just as effective as drugs are. The reason for this lies in bacteria.

The Gut is a house to billions of microorganisms (micro bios); it is a place where they live and thrive. These micro bios perform crucial functions that the body can't perform on its own. There are more species of them in the gut than anywhere else in the body. However, most of them are either ***firmicutes*** or ***bacteroidetes***, which make-up 75 percent of them. The micro bios can be good or bad.

Most of the micro bios in the gut are good. However, sometimes, bad ones often get mixed in. Nevertheless, this isn't a challenge as the body ensures they are in the right balance. But considering the fact that stress and change of diet can result in a change in good bacteria. At this stage, it can result in many negative health effects. The changes in bacterial balance or population also often results in the alteration of brain chemicals. Hence, this results in symptoms of mental illnesses.

The same way gut can affect brain chemicals, the brain can also damage gut bacteria. With just a few hours of psychological stress, the balance of the micro bios in the gut will be altered. The ANS and the HPA axis send signals to the gut bacteria when one is stressed, causing a change in bacteria composition and behavior. This consequently leaves one exposed to harm. The brain can also determines how the guts contracts, controls the secretion of acid (which provides the gut's protection), and other physical movements of the gut. When the brain isn't functioning well, the gut's normal functioning is compromised, food isn't properly absorbed, and the body becomes affected.

The gut needs the brain to be stable and healthy so as to produce the right balance of chemical bacteria. Conversely, the brain needs the right balance of gut bacteria to produce the right balance it requires to be healthy. An unhealthy gut results in an unhealthy brain and vice versa. An April 2019 survey carried out in 1000 people shows that butyrate-producing bacteria was linked to higher quality of life in people. It was found to be in lower measures in people with depression. The survey also proved that GABA production was also minimal in people with depression.

Food impact the brain through its influence on gut bacteria. Some food helps in the production of healthy bacteria, while others impede it. Consequently, food is one of the most effective mental health medicine available. When food is broken down, its components can influence neurotransmitters like serotonin, GABA, dopamine, etc. which then flows to the brain to change the way one thinks and/or feels. Food is particularly most impactful on the brain through its influence on the gut bacteria. It can lead to the production or inhibition of healthy gut bacteria. This is why it (food) is one of the most important "drug" available to address mental illnesses, at a cheaper rate (compared to pharmaceuticals) and with fewer side effects.

Naidoo argues that psychiatry and the medical world as a whole have paid excessive emphasis on symptoms alone without attention to the nutrition and lifestyle of their patients. Hey have assumed that psychiatric problems rest solely in the brain, with no statistical validity. She argues that the problem is bigger than psychiatry and we have to examine the patients and their life style as a whole. This is exacerbated by the fact that medical schools and residency programs don't train students on how to speak to their patients about their dietary choices.

Thankfully, the new phase of healthcare where prescriptions isn't just about medicines: patients are more empowered than ever. While a better diet is important, it is only one approach to treating mental illnesses. Hence, seeking professional, getting enough sleep, practicing mindfulness, etc. are equally important.

Chapter 2: Depression, Probiotics, Omega-3s, and the Mediterranean eating pattern

Here, Naidoo examines how food can be used to heal bad moods. She draws an inseparable link between depression and poor diet. She notes that depression or bad moods naturally cause people to turn to junk foods. Depression often makes people make poor food choices. She cites a 2018 Cross Sectional Research on depressed college students which shows that 30.3 percent of them ate fried foods, 49 percent of them drank sweetened drinks, and 51.8 percent ate sugary foods.

Besides, depression has been found to cause people make poor food choices. This is due to the fact that it is associated with decreasing mood-regulating neurotransmitters like serotonin. Wanting to feel better is naturally linked to the craving for sweetened foods and drinks. However, it turns out that high sugar intake turn out to worsen depression, increasing the chances of a recurrence. However, there are foods that can boost moods. This partly owes to the relationship between the gut and the brain.

Naidoo notes that food can change the kind of bacteria in the guts, affecting the balance of the good and bad bacteria. Food can also influence the kinds of chemicals they send to the brain. Recent studies have also shown that bacteria species linked to higher life qualities are depleted in patients of depression, while inflammation-causing bacteria are found in higher numbers in them.

Naidoo argues that gut-induced depressions can be addressed with the use of prebiotics and prebiotics in diet. ***Probiotics*** are live bacteria that provide health benefits to the body and brain, when eaten. A 2017 study from the University Of Virginia School Of Medicine shows that *Lactobacillus*, which is a component in human probiotics, reduced depression in rats. Recent studies have reflected the same in humans.

Prebiotics **(note: Not probiotics)** are food for healthy bacteria; they are kinds of fiber that our bodies cannot digest, and meant for only the good bacteria in our body. To be effective, probiotics break down prebiotic to form short-chain fatty acids that help block the growth of cancer cells, while helping the growth of healthy cells. Probiotics can be increased through dietary sources like yoghourts (but not those high in added sugars), fermented soya bean products, soured yoghourt, fermented tea drink, butter milk, etc. Prebiotic rich foods include beans and other legumes, oats, garlic, onions, berries, leaks.

There are a few other ways by which foods can affect moods. In order to improve mood, and get rid of depression, avoid the following food substances:

Sugar: The more sugar one eats, they more likely they are to be depressed. This is because, to function well, the brain makes use of a type of sugar glucose. Now, it only needs 62 grams of glucose over a period of 24 hours. Excessive glucose can culminate in inflammation in the brain, consequently resulting in depression.

High Glycemic Load Carbohydrates: Even though high carbohydrate food like bread, pasta, etc. made from flour may not taste sweet, they are processed the same way the body processes sugar. This is why the quality of carbs we take matter. Better quality carbohydrates are defined as grains, food high in fiber, and those that rank low on the Glycemic Index GI.

High GI foods are foods quickly converted to glucose when digested. High GI carbs are some of the common causes of depression. They include white rice, potatoes, white rice. Medium GI carbs include honey, whole-wheat bread, and orange juice. Low GI foods include green vegetables, kidney beans, raw carrots, lentils, etc. You do not need to cut out carbs completely, but to choose the right ones in reasonable measures.

Studies show that people who consume low GI carbs are less likely to develop depression compared to people who consume high GI carbs.

Artificial Sweeteners: Food manufacturers often use sweeteners like saccharin, aspartame, NutraSweet, sucralose, splenda, truvia, stevia, etc. in their products. Studies show that these artificial sweeteners can be toxic to the brain, and may result in depression. Studies have shown that people who consume drinks with artificial sweeteners are more depressed than those who don't.

Aspartame, which is popular in man diet drinks, has been found by a 2017 study to increase some substances in the brain which impedes the release of happy neurotransmitters like dopamine, noradrenaline, and serotonin. Also, it causes oxidation (which increases harmful free radicals in the brain, unstable molecules which damages the cells).

Sucralose has also been linked to depression, by altering gut bacteria. However, not all sweeteners are known to be harmful.

Fried Foods: Minimizing the amount of fried foods in diets is an important step to avoiding fried foods. A study in Japan that aimed at examine the level of depression and resilience in factory workers found that those who consumed more fried foods were more likely to develop depression. If one ate fried foods daily, Naidoo prescribes switching to weekly; if weekly, once a month. What matters is to avoid consuming them.

Bad Fats: Most fried foods are fried with unhealthy fats. Some examples of this unhealthy fats include margarine and hydrogenated oils. Good fats like avocadoes, almonds and olive oils that are healthy are rarely used.

Added Nitrates: They are used to preserve and to add color to foods like meats and sausages. They can also alter gut bacteria, leading to depression or bipolar disorder.

The following are foods to eat to promote good moods:

Foods rich in Omega-3 fatty acids: They play a very crucial roles in mental health, and serve as a vital part of cell membranes. They produce the hormones that regulated blood clotting, traction, inflammation of artery walls. The body cannot produce them. Hence, we depend on means to produce them. The three main Omega-3s are:

Alpha-linolenic acid (ALA)

Eicosapentaenoic acid (EPA

Docosahexaenoic acid (DHA).

These are all important to the body. Most studies show that they are important to fighting depression. Eating foods rich in Omega-3s such as fatty fish, walnuts, vegetable oils, etc. are effective against depression. The best source of Omega-3s of these is fish.

<u>Foods rich in helpful vitamins</u>: Certain vitamins have been associated with the maintenance of good moods. Examples are vitamin B9 and B12. A deficiency in these vitamins results in the loss of brain cells, leading to depression. Vitamins B1 and B6 and C also play fundamental roles. Deficiency in Vitamin A can also result in a shrinkage of the brain area, thus affecting how the brain responds to stress.

<u>Food rich in iron and other helpful minerals</u>: Iron makes up the part of the brain that protect neurons. It controls the synthesis of mood-controlling chemicals pathways. Some good sources of iron include shell fish, legumes, pumpkin seeds, dark chocolates lean red meat and organ meats (in moderation). Other minerals like magnesium, potassium, zinc, etc. are also important.

<u>Seasonings, spices and herbs</u>: Spices have anti-oxidant properties which prevent oxidative stress which prevents depression. They can be combined with other anti-oxidant foods for better effectiveness. They help the brain fight-off harmful free radicals and help prevent oxidative stress. They include Oxygen Radical Absorbent Capacities (ORAC), saffron, turmeric, oregano, etc. They have all been found to be effective against depression.

It may be difficult to remember which foods are higher in which nutrients while you stand at a grocery store. Given this, the best approach is to follow a broad diet that helps to promote your moods. Such diet exist. They are:

The Mediterranean Eating Pattern (MEP)

Even though the Mediterranean diet isn't created with mental health in mind, it features the healthy components listed above in their appropriate balance. It is also healthy for the body in many other ways. Daily foods of the Mediterranean meals should include 3 to 9 servings of vegetables, ½ to 2 servings of fruits, 1 to 13 servings of cereals, breads and other grains, 8 servings of olive oil. All these amount in 2200 calories of total fat.

Studies have shown that the MEP protects against diabetes, heart disease, and confers longevity. It is also known to be effective against depressive symptoms.

Some other traditional eating patterns may be helpful. The Norwegian Diet (also called the Nordic diet) is a key example. It prioritizes plant foods over meat and animal products. The Japanese Diet is another example.

Chapter 3: Anxiety, Fermented foods, Dietary Fiber and the Tryptophan Myth

Here, Naidoo links feelings of anxiety with the gut. This feelings have been built into our language with expressions like "butterflies in one's stomach" for nervousness or "pit in the stomach" for feelings of dread. This proves the link between the gut and the brain. She notes that imbalances in the gut causes of Generalized Anxiety Disorders, a condition that makes regular daily worries to feel overwhelming. It takes the form of panic disorders, social anxiety disorder, agoraphobia, and etc. Though these conditions develop in different ways and triggered by specific factors, they affect the brain in such a way that they cause panic attacks. Anxiety disorders are the most common psychiatric cases in the US.

Now, while there are different ways of treating anxiety, only 50% to 60% of the people respond to treatment, and only a quarter of patients experience a complete resolution of their symptoms. A fundamental way of addressing them is through diets.

A part of the brain that is directly influenced by changes in the gut micro bio is the amygdala. It is an important part of the brain socket that goes awry when one is anxious. The connection between the amygdala and the gut is so strong that some researchers believe that anxiety can be reduced in the brain by targeted changes in the gut micro bio.

As a result of the direct connection between the gut and the brain, there is a correlation between anxiety and bowel disorders. About 60% of people suffering from anxiety have Irritable Bowel Syndrome (IBS), a chronic disorder which causes abdominal pain and changes in bowel habits without any obvious cause. It manifest in the forms of gassing, diarrhea, bloating, etc. Usually, the IBS is only as severe as the anxiety. IBS also affects the part of the brain that is responsible for task management, pain management, and feel emotions.

Anxiety is also common in people with Inflammatory Bowel Disease (IBD), which features bowel disorders (causing structural damage to the gut). About 40 percent of people suffer from these disorders.

Here are some foods to avoid in getting rid of anxiety:

The Western Diet: This describes the standard American diet - meals commonly found in fast food meals. They contained lots of bad fats, red meat, and sweetened drinks. Among several negative effects this has on the body, anxiety takes a center stage.

Studies have shown that high carb diets lead to obesity and anxiety. A 2016 study shows that rats on high fat diets were more prone to diabetes and anxiety. Also lower carb diets was said to decrease anxiety in mice while also increasing brain blood flow.

It is believed that it causes brain serotonin to be reduced in some parts, thus leading to anxiety. It can also lead to obesity (which causes mood and obesity disorders). However, while it is important to cut down fats and carbs, it's important to not get excessive.

Caffeine: While this may be particularly useful in a busy world, excess amounts of it can lead to anxiety or worsen it. Some studies show that caffeine activate the mid-brain periaqueductal gray matter, a part of the brain that is usually activated when pursued by a predator; it also stops the part of the brain responsible for managing anxiety. One may not have to get-rid of caffeine totally, but can consider cutting down, and stay under 400ml daily consumption.

Alcohol: Heavy drinking may provide temporary relaxation but often results in feelings of guilt and anxiety. Besides, it is one of the leading causes of death in the US. Men who drink more than fourteen drink a week or more than four drinks a day are considered heavy drinkers. Similarly, women who drink more than seven drinks per week and three drinks per day are considered heavy drinkers. To break free from heavy drinking, one can develop a plan to quit alcohol. This can be effective with the help of a psychologist or doctor.

Gluten: Studies on excessive gluten consumption have proven that it can lead to celiac disease. People who go on gluten-free diets have been found to experience less anxiety than they experienced before cutting off gluten.

Artificial Sweeteners: Artificial sweeteners can result in bad gut bacteria, which can affect the brain. They are better minimized in diets.

Here are foods that help fight anxiety:

Dietary fiber: Some studies have proven that foods rich in dietary fiber helps with the reduction of anxiety and stress. They can only be broken down by good bacteria in the gut, thus leading to their increase. This ultimately improves mood and help with anxiety alleviation.

Since fiber-rich foods often take time to chew, one tends to eat them more slowly. Thus, the body has ample time to recognize it is full. It helps in keeping weight down, and also decreasing inflammation throughout the body by calming down the brain and body inflammatory responses. Some dietary fiber foods include the *Five Bs* – beans, brown rice, berries, bran, and baked potatoes with the skin on. Others high fiber foods are, carrots, apples, bananas, almonds, walnuts, oats, etc.

Omega-3s: A 2011 study carried out to test the effect of Omega-3s on sixty-nine medical students to measure their anxiety levels during lower stress periods and in exams, students who were given more omega-3s had 20% less anxiety than those who weren't. They also had 14% less inflammation in their bodies. Some other recent studies studies have also shown that Omega-3s are associated with anxiety reductions due to its anti-inflammatory and neurochemical influence on the brain.

Aged, fermented and cultured foods: Fermented foods have been linked helpful bacteria which facilitate healthy gut functions and decrease anxiety. A 2015 study on 710 people regarding their fermented food consumption shows that eating fermented food regularly reduced symptoms of social anxiety in neurotic or unstable patients. Yoghurts without added sugar and Kimchee are examples of fermented foods.

Tryptophan (TRP): Since TRP is a precursor of serotonin, scientists have argues that it could raise serotonin levels to cure anxiety. A 2014 study carried out on 25 healthy persons show that individuals who consume more TRP had lesser depression, irritability and anxiety. However, only purified TRPs can help raise serotonin levels; foods containing TRPs cannot. Being the least abundant amino acids in protein, it can easily be crowded out by other amino acids that can prevent it from access into the brain. However, eating carbohydrates along with protein tend to increase the chances of tryptophan's access to the brain. Turkey, other meats and chickpeas – especially when combined with carbohydrates – are reliable sources.

Vitamin D: Some studies have shown that Vitamin D made people less depressed and anxious. It is recognized as a neurosteroid. This is because it crosses the blood/brain barrier, entering brain cells and decreasing inflammation and cell destruction. About 85% percent of vitamin D come from the exposure of the skin too sunlight. Other sources are fortified milk, egg yolk, salmon, sundried mushrooms, etc.

Other vitamins (like Vitamins A, C, and E) are also necessary for sustaining a good mood by protecting the brain from toxins, boost immunities and regulate mood chemicals in the brain. In several studies, multivitamins were found effective against stress and anxiety.

Magnesium: A 2017 study reveals that magnesium can change the levels of stress chemicals in the brain, as a result of which it eases anxiety. It also helps muscles relax after contracting. Hence, low magnesium can result in prolonged contraction, resulting in muscle cramps and tightness. Magnesium-rich foods include almonds, spinach, peanuts, cashew, cooked black beans, peanut butter, and avocado, etc.

Nutritional and Herbal Supplements: A 2010 study shows that herbal supplements and spices like Persian flower, guava, turmeric, lavender oil, chamomile etc. helps to reduce anxiety. One advantage they have over is that they cause less sedation (which is frequent with pharmaceutical products). Also, staying hydrated is also an important part of keeping anxiety in check and to stay healthy.

Chapter 4: PTSD, Glutamate, Blueberries, and Old Friends Bacteria

In this chapter, Naidoo presents the most effective ways diets can be used to manage PTSD symptoms. PTSD occurs when one encounters a traumatic event like natural disaster, difficult break-up, sexual assault, etc. Most people who experience traumatic events do not develop PTSD. However, those who do experience it for a long time; it may even recur years after the traumatic events. It often manifests symptoms like recurrent memories of the traumatic events, disturbed dreams, overreacting to normal events, etc. These symptoms occur as a result of *excessive amygdala activation* and lack of activity in the frontal cortex or hippocampus, which play key roles in memory, fear response, and trauma-processing.

Traumatic events usually trigger the brain's "fight or flight" system through the HPA axis which causes the instinct determine how to deal with them. PTSD creates constant disruption in the HPA axis when it causes traumatic events to repeat again and again.

Since the HPA axis is one of the channels between the gut and the brain, it means the gut is not spared from trauma. PTSD has one of the strongest brain-body relationships causing wear and tear on the body coupled with a number mental symptoms. PTSD thus creates symptoms lead to wear and tear on the body, leading to stomach ulcers, bowel disruptions, gull-bladder disorders, etc. It also results in brain inflammation.

A 2018 study shows that types of gut bacteria in people exposed to trauma were similar, whether or not they developed PTSD. However, people with PTSD had fewer ***actinobacteria***, ***lentisphaerae***, and ***verrucomicrobia*** which have been considered "old friends" of the human body. The old friend hypothesis holds that humans lived, in olden societies, in a way that promoted these beneficial bacteria which protected us from inflammatory diseases. However, with urbanization, humans do not interact with these bacteria any longer, leading to increase in these diseases and limiting inflammation in the brain.

The following are foods that can worsen PTSD:

High-fat diets: Diets rich in unhealthy fats like saturated fat, trans-fat and fats (used in fried foods rather than healthy fats like omega-3s or those found in olive oil) are unhealthy. People who take high-fat diets are more susceptible to PTSD. A key way for people going through PTSD to improve their diets is to think about their comfort foods as an addiction they have to overcome to preserve their brains and feel less anxious.

Sugar and High GI carbs: A 2010 study on Bosnia war refugees shows that people with PTSD make people more vulnerable to metabolic disorders like diabetes. This may also increase their PTSD symptoms. This is because high blood sugar affects the capacity of the hippocampus to react to stress. However, it's apt to note that sweet foods aren't the only suspect here.

High GI carbs like white rice, potatoes, and white bread can also increase blood sugar. Nevertheless, while knowing each food GI index is important, combined or mixed meals can also have different effects. For instance, a study has shown that rice, being a naturally having a high GI index, results into a low GI index when it is combined with egg, beans, sesame oil.

Glutamate: It is used to increase food flavor in foods, and creates a unique taste called "umami." It is not recognizable as sweetness, bitterness, sourness, etc. It is an entirely different taste (the sixth basic taste for humans). Umami taste is most commonly imparted in foods with the use of Monosodium Glutamate (MSG).

Some studies have shown that MSG can cause problems like brain toxicity in sensitive individuals. Hence, it can worsen PTSD symptoms in patients. Tomato sauce, tomato sauce, miso, savory snack, chips, etc. are examples of foods with glutamate. One may not have to cut out glutamate completely but to minimize it.

The following are some foods that can help sooth effects of PTSD, and get brains back to normal functions:

Blueberries: A 2016 study on rats shows that blueberries-rich diets increase serotonin levels in the brain and reduced inflammation. Adding ½ to 1 cup of blueberries to one's diet a day could prove really healthy, as long as they don't have added sugar or preservatives.

Omega-3 fatty acids: A 2019 study shows that omega-3s protected the brain (especially the hippocampus) in rats with PTSD. Another 2013 study on 300 people shows that the higher the level of Omega-3s in people, the lower the levels of PTSD. Fish – particularly fatty fishes like salmon, sardines, tuna, etc. are the richest sources of them. Plant oil (like canola and soya bean oils), grass-fed beef, egg, milk, yoghurt, etc. are other example of foods rich in omega-3s. A vegetarian can take organic Panola oils and other foods rich in omega-3s.

Vitamin E: Free radicals (which are harmful to the brain by causing oxidative stress) can come from inflammation or stress. They can also stem from exposure to X-rays, Cigarette smoke, industrial chemicals, etc. These can damage the cells in the body the same way stress can.

Vitamin E is a defense system against free radicals which prevents brain damage. A daily table spoon of wheat germ oil can be sufficient. Other sources include sun flower seeds, raw tomatoes, peanut butters, etc.

Spices and Natural Supplements: Spices such as ginkgo biloba, black pepper, and turmeric can also be effective against PTSD symptoms.

Chapter 5: ADHD, Gluten, Milk Caseins and Phenols

In this chapter, Naidoo presents the most effective way of addressing the Attention Deficit Hyperactivity Disorder (ADHD), which shows symptoms such as difficulty paying attention, hyperactivity, and impulsivity. Different patients may experience different kinds of symptoms experience. Unstable moods, anxiety, difficulty learning are often primary. It mostly begins at childhood but can also be found in adults, and can last for years.

Unlike several other conditions, it is more common in children, even though several adults also suffer from it. This makes it similar to other cases like Sensory Processing Disorder and Autism Spectrum Disorder. However, healthy diets can effectively address the condition both in children and adults.

ADHD has been found to affect the connection between different brain regions like the prefrontal cortex, which is known as the thinking brain, and the striatum, which deals with reward behaviors. It also affects the brain's chemistry; especially the levels of dopamine and the noradrenaline (the flight or fight hormone). Dopamine and noradrenaline are naturally unable to cross the blood/brain barrier. However, they are made of smaller molecules that can. Now, these smaller molecules are made in the gut. Hence, the gut is also affected in the process.

The bacteria in the gut produce different brain chemicals. Hence, a change in gut bacteria can result in a chemical imbalance in the brain. The connection of the gut explains why ADHD can manifest gastro-intestinal symptoms like constipation.

The following are foods that can worsen ADHD:

<u>Gluten</u>: ADHD has been linked with Gluten Intolerance or Celiac disease. A 2006 study shows that people with celiac disease were more likely to have ADHD and that a celiac-free diet helped them improve. However, one doesn't have to have celiac disease to be sensitive to gluten. This is called **non-celiac gluten sensitivity**. The link between celiac disease and the brain is not fully understood.

Dairy: Diary contains a lot of casein. Hence, to consume a lot of dairy means consuming a lot of casein (which worsens ADHD). Casein is found in dairy products like cheese, yoghurts, ice creams, etc.

Sugar: Even tough Sugar doesn't cause ADHD, it can have effect on it by increasing adrenaline, thus increasing blood sugar levels, which, in turn leads to hyperactivity. Since it also reduces dopamine sensitivity in the brain, it can increase impulsive reward-seeking behavior.

Food colorings and additives: Studies have shown that they contain salicylates. Hence it has been linked to making students more restless and inattentive. A 2012 and 2017 meta-analysis showed that the elimination of coloring and additives benefited children with ADHD.

Here are foods that can help fight ADHD:

Mediterranean Eating Patterns: Some studies have shown that MEP address ADHD symptoms, and helps avoid it. This pattern has already been discussed in chapter two. Asides this pattern, taking nutrient-enriched breakfasts also play key roles.

Caffeine: even though it helps to increase people's motivation, alertness, efficiency, vigilance, attention, etc., it is important not to take excess of it. 400ml of caffeine for adults is fine. It's safe to keep it off children.

Polyphenols: A 2018 study shows dietary polyphenols can be useful in addressing oxalated stress on the brain, thus improve ADHD symptoms and to prevent brain cell damage. It can also exert other helpful biological effects like helping the generation of neurons. Some sources of polyphenols are berries, cherries, eggplants, onions, green teas, etc.

Dietary Micronutrients: Some studies show that deficiency of zinc, vitamin C, vitamin B iron and magnesium, etc. is often responsible for ADHD in children.

Chapter 6: Dementia and Brain Fog: Micro greens, Rosemary and the Mind Diet

Dementia

In this chapter, Naidoo presents how diet can be used to preserve memory and to clear the mind from brain fog. Dementia comes in very forms. Vascular dementia often occurs due to blood vessel blockages which stop blood from feeding brain tissue. Frontal temporal dementia are a general brain issues that cause memory loss. Others forms are less well-understood. She notes that food can also be effective against dementia and its different causes.

Naidoo argues that the gut and the memory connection isn't hard to note. It is responsible for bowel reactions to certain memories or experiences. This shows that the gut works with the brain's memory system. This connection lies in certain chemicals which are regulated by the gut and which make the body and brain function. A change in gut bacteria can thus affect the levels of cortisol, which in turn can affect memory.

Another evidence of the connection of gut and memory is the fact that the composition of gut bacteria changes in patients of several memory-related diseases. Hence, a way of reducing the possibility of dementia is to reduce food that harm gut bacteria and by eating foods that enhance them.

In order to know which foods are helpful to memory, it's important to note that there are several memory systems in the brain. They are ***Procedural memory systems*** (which helps to learn tasks or skills), ***Relational memory*** (which helps to recall facts or events), and ***Working memory*** (useful for short-term remembering).

The following are foods that weaken memory:

The Western Diet: High fat and high GI foods have been found to affect neurons in the hippocampus (which is responsible for relational memories). It can also affect the pre-frontal cortex, causing information to travel more slowly. This consequently affects memory. Cutting down on high fat and sugar as well as exercising regularly improves memory.

Gluten: Several cases of dementia are associated with celiac disease and non-celiac gluten sensitivity. Patients who have celiac disease often experience sudden memory losses. It also tends to lead to dementia.

Protecting Memory through Diet

How eating can fight dementia

Calorie restriction: Eating calories overall seems to have negative effect on memory. A 2009 study showed that restricting calorie by 35 percent improve memory. Other studies have linked improved memory to low insulin and excessive protein.

Soy: Studies show that soy improve memory and cognition. Soy beans and products are rich in isoflavones which improves memory. A 2015 study carried on 1024 proves that soy isoflavones improved cognitive functions and visual memory in post-menopausal women.

Alcohol: A 2018 study shows that red wine have an impact on memory improvement in men. Other studies show that light alcohol use decrease the chances of developing dementia. However, heavy use may increase its risk.

Coffee: A 2017 study on several elderly men shows that men who took 3 to 5 cups of coffee had lower risk of dementia. This is because coffee protects brain blood vessels, prevents tissues damage and brain vessel blockage. However, not all substance in coffee is helpful. Some substance may increase cholesterol levels, thus leading to the thickening and the hardening of the walls of the brain. This is why it is important consume moderately.

Olive Oil: Some studies have shown that extra virgin olive oil (EVOO) is a source of compounds which have strong antioxidant properties which acts as antioxidants and brain protectors.

Spices: Turmeric pepper, rosemary, ginger, curry, etc. have all also been found to be helpful to memory.

Researchers have come up with a diet that incorporates all food supplements that are healthy for improving memory - the MIND diet.

MIND stands for **Mediterranean-Dash Intervention for Neurodegenerative Delay**. It comprises two diets: the Mediterranean and the DASH diet.

The Mediterranean diet is already discussed in chapter 2. Its key features is the fact that it is low in saturated fat, high in healthy oil, with red meats eaten rarely. The MIND diet has also been linked with memory protection and the reduction of the risk of Parkinson's disease.

DASH stands for **Dietary Approach to Stop Hypertension**. DASH diet involves five servings of vegetables, five servings of fruits, five servings of carbs, two servings of fat of low-fay dairy products, two or fewer servings of lean meat, two to three times of nuts and seeds. These are vital against cognitive decline.

Green leafy vegetables – 6 or more servings per week.

Other vegetables (green and red peppers, squash, carrots, tomato sauce, eggplant, etc.) – 1 or more servings a day.

Berries (strawberries, blackberries, blueberries, etc.) – 2 or more servings per week

Nuts – 5 or more servings per week

Olive oil – Used as primary oil

Whole grains – 3 or more servings per day

Fish (Omega-3) – One or more meals per week. Not fried.

Beans – More than 3 weeks per week

Chicken or Turkey – 2 or more wills per week

Wine – One glass per day.

Brain Fog

Brain Fog is another condition that can cause gaps in cognition. It occurs when one is unable to think clearly, concentrate or multitask. It is linked to the loss of short term and long term memory. It is common in patients of early Alzheimer's disease, Autism spectrum disorder, chromium fatigue syndrome, etc. Researchers have linked its causes to excessive brain inflammation. It can be addressed with diets similar to the Mediterranean Eating Pattern or the MIND diet.

The following are foods that are effective against brain fog:

Laureolum: A 2015 study shows that laureolum has antioxidant and inflammatory substances that decrease brain fog and prevents toxic destruction of nerve cells in the brain. Foods that have laureolum includes fresh peppermint, thyme, celery seeds, dry Mexican oregano, etc.

Note: The use of probiotics and gluten may, however, be harmful as they can result in brain fog.

Phosphatidylserine (PS): This is required for healthy cell membraines. It can protect the brain from brain fog. It is found in soy beans, white beans, eggs and dairy products.

Citicoline: Studies show that it is vital in addressing dopamine depletion. It is contained in beef liver and egg yolks.

Chapter 7: Obsessive Compulsive Disorder: Nach, Glycine, and the Dangers of Orthorexia Nervosa

In this chapter, Naidoo examines Obsessive Compulsive Disorder (OCD) and how it can be addressed with diets. OCD is the cause of unending (often unreasonable) worries about regular things. For many years, it was classified an anxiety disorder. However, of recent, it has become categorized under the OCD spectrum. People with OCD suffer Generalized Anxiety Disorder, Body Dimorphic Disorders, Trichotillomania, Excoriation Disorder, skin picking, pathological gambling, Kleptomania, Sexual Compulsivity, etc.

Change in gut bacteria often result in OCD and worsens it. Similarly, gut bacteria changes with OCD symptoms. A survey showed that people who used probiotics experienced limited OCD symptoms. Some researchers have argued that OCD symptoms have linked OCD symptoms to the connection between the gut and the brain. Hence, drugs or food substances in the gut can alter the balance of the microbes in the gut and trigger OCD symptoms.

The following are foods that can worsen OCD:

Glutamate: This has already been discussed in chapter four. While it is fine when consumed in smaller amounts, it is dangerous for OCD sufferers. However, there are two types of dietary glutamate:

Bound glutamate is usually eaten as a protein, as a result of which it can be digested well. Free glutamate, on the other hand, can cause spikes of glutamate in the blood. This makes it dangerous. **Free glutamate** can be found in food substances like cured meat, Roquefort, parmesan cheese, soy sauce, ripe tomatoes, fish sauce, grape juice, cheese etc.

Gluten: A 2018 study found the removal of gluten caused OCD sufferers to be less distressed. The reason for this are however not well established.

The following are foods and supplements that can fight OCD:

N-acetylcysteine (NAC): It is used to treat several non-mental health challenges. Studies have shown that it is effective against OCD spectrum disorder. It inhibits the release of glutamate in nerve cells and many brain regions, thus helping to reduce OCD risk. It has been particularly found helpful against compulsive nail biting and skin picking behavior. Meat, grains, eggs, red pepper, onions, are foods that contain NAC.

Myo-inositol (MI): It is a variant of glucose made naturally in the body, but can be consumed through food. It has been found efficacious against OCDs. However, it has been linked to mild gastro-intestinal side effects like diarrhea, nausea, flatulence. It is found in fruits, beans, nuts, citrus fruits, and grains. It can also be found found in fresh carrots, peanut butters, vegetables, etc.

Glycine: Studies have shown that glycine may be effective against OCDs as it interacts with the glutamate receptor, NMDA receptor, found in the brain. A 2009 study shows that it is highly effective against serious OCD symptoms. Glycine is present in dairy products, bananas, leghumes, meats, fish, turkey, etc.

Milk thistle (Silybum Marianum): It is a flower which is used as a medicinal plant. It contains a substance called the "flavonoid silymarin" which serves as natural de-oxidant. Among other functions, it removes serotonin from the brain, thus easing OCD symptoms. It is found in cylibum marianum.

Vitamin B12: It is essential for the production of brain chemicals like serotonin. Studies have also showed Vitamin B12 curing patients of OCD symptoms.

Curcumin: It is found in turmeric. A 2012 study shows that it is found to influence serotonin, dopamine, and noradrenaline metabolism. It has been found to impact serotonin, noradrenaline, and dopamine metabolisms. It is thus found impactful against OCD symptoms.

Special Considerations

Orthorexia Nervosa. This refers to unhealthy obsession to weight control diets. It is safer to begin with one food at a time, start with the least-restrictive change, plan ahead, and measure weight weekly rather than daily. These are healthy for people with OCD tendencies.

Muscle dysmorphia: This refers to an obsession with compulsive exercise. To prevent this, one has to avoid radical diet changes, consult a doctor when making diet changes, avoid supplements from unreliable sources, and be wary of underlined psychological consequences. OCD can begin with a seeming healthy desire.

Chapter 8: Insomnia and Fatigue: Capsaicin, Chamomile, and Anti-inflammatory Diet

Insomnia

Here, Naidoo appraises sleeping disorders and fatigue and how they can be addressed with dietary changes. She notes that close to 1/3 of the world's population have trouble sleeping (insomnia). This tends to affect key organ in the body like the brain, heart, lung, etc.

The gut-brain relationship plays a key role here: maintaining the right balance of bacteria in the gut is crucial to getting sleep. This is because of the fact that gut bacteria plays key roles in the brain. This is because gut bacteria communicates with the brain to determine sleep processes. Also, when one is sleep deprived or sleep circle is altered, the gut chemicals and metabolism is affected. This can affect how one metabolizes food which may result in obesity or overweight.

Diet has also been found to play a key role in how one sleeps. How one eats or the kinds of food that one eats determines how they sleep and how satisfying they sleep. For instance, excess protein intake has been linked with difficulty maintaining sleep.

The following are foods that disrupt sleep:

Caffeine: Caffeine is often consumed to prevent sleep. This owes to the fact that it acts on "adenosine receptors" in the brain - responsible for sleep, cognition and arousal. This is why they are very active against sleep.

Now, eliminating caffeine may not be the perfect step to take since there some benefits to it. Hence, it is ideal to only use it moderately and wisely. Drinking three to four cups a day is fine. Also avoiding them late in the day is safer.

Alcohol: Alcohol has been found to hurt sleep more than it is assumed to help. Studies have shown that people who have a habit of using alcohol tend to have more troubles with sleep than those who don't. This is because it tends to activate the amygdala and worsening anxiety. Trying to abstain for a while can be just apt.

The following are foods that aid sleep:

Omega-3s: Improved sleep has been linked to omega-3s (unsaturated fatty acids). This owes to the fact that it prevents inflammation, protecting the brain from sleep-depriving factors, just the same way it works against depression, anxiety, etc. It also helps to develop melatonin.

Melatonin: It is a hormone in the brain which aids sleep. Studies have shown that it can be vital for sleep, which can be very useful for people going through seasonal depression (often by regulating their sleep cycles). Melatonin is available as a supplement but is also available in foods like fish, egg, milk, fruits, nuts, sunflower seeds, mustard seeds, tomatoes, cucumber, rice and other grains.

Tryptophan: It has also been linked to improved sleep. This is because it increases brain serotonin and melatonin which are vital sleep-aiding agents. However, it is safer to take it under the supervision of a doctor. Turkey, meats, chickpeas, especially when combined with carbohydrates, are great sources of tryptophan.

L-Ornithine: This is an essential amino acids that cannot be produced by the body which is also highly beneficial to sleep. It is gotten from food sources. It has the capacity to improve sleep. It is produced from foods containing l-arginine, which comes from protein sources. Meats, eggs, poultry, fish, soya beans, etc.

Chamomile: It is most commonly used as a sleep aid. A 2016 study found that it improves sleep significantly. The most common way to get it is to take chamomile tea. However, it is important to consult a doctor before using chamomile as it can interact with pain killers, sedatives, etc. Besides, some patients may react to it. Lettuce, cherry juice, lingzhi, are examples of foods with Chamomile,

Other Micronutrients: Some other compounds that are beneficial to sleep include GABA, calcium, potassium, etc. They can be found in cherries, lingzhi, lettuce, placebo, etc.

Fatigue

When one isn't sleeping well, there is a high tendency of feeling fatigued. Nevertheless, fatigue has been linked to a few other causes. It is important to consult a doctor to ascertain the exact cause. But, generally, it can be addressed with the right diet.

The following are some food substances that fight fatigue:

Anti-inflammatory foods: Inflammation is one of the main causes of fatigue. Anti-inflammatory diets thus can be effective. Since the brain is made up of 60% fat, enough omega-3 fatty acids would prove vital. These fatty acids are found in corn, sun flower, nuts, grape seeds, peanuts, and vegetables. It is also important to avoid fast foods. Polyphenols like coco powders, Mexican oregano, chestnut, black chocolate, green teas, cinnamon, black berries, grape seeds, etc. can also help to reduce inflammation. Plant-based foods and vegetables also play a key role.

Magnesium and Zinc: Researchers have discovered that fatigue is linked to low magnesium in the red blood cell. Magnesium is found in food sources like dry roasted almonds, cooked black beans, dry roasted cashews, etc. Zinc deficiency is also another common cause of fatigue. It is found in lamb, pumpkin seeds, grass-fed beef, and chickpeas.

Vitamins B6, B12, C, D, and E: They protect the brain while energizing the body. They can be gotten through natural sources like meat, fish, eggs, vegetables and fruits.

Capsaicin: This is a substance in chili peppers which makes them spicy. It has been found to supply the body with energy.

Black cumin (Nigella sativa seed): Studies show that black cumin is neuro-protective due to its anti-oxidant properties. It is also proven to aid in muscle contraction.

Chapter 9: Bipolar Disorder and Schizophrenia: L-theanine, Healthy Fats, and the Ketogenic Diet

Here, Naidoo examines Bipolar Disorder (BD) and Schizophrenia (SCZ), and how they can be addressed with diets. BD and SCZ have been found to be among the most popular psychiatric disorders. Patients who suffer from Bipolar Disorder experience dramatic mood changes often on a weekly basis. Schizophrenia symptoms are classified into positive and negative. Positive symptoms are those which include psychotic behavior like illusions and hallucinations.

Negative symptoms are those that alter behavior. Examples are gobbled speech, looking withdrawn and depressed. BD is classified as a mood disorder, while SCZ is classified as a psychotic disorder. However, BD sometimes shows psychotic behaviors like hallucination, making it difficult to specify. SCZ, on the other hand, may display some mood symptoms like being irritable, which may be seen as a symptom of BD. This is why some researchers believe that SCZ doesn't exist or that both BD and SZC exist in the same spectrum.

Bipolar Disorder

A common symptom of BD is the fact that mood is prone to dramatic changes. People with BD can get so alert, talk so fast, etc. After a week or more, they plunge into depression, with no interest in regular activities. People with BD often suffer from a number of other medical issues. For instance, obesity is often linked to people with BD. They also often have diabetes, cardiovascular disease, autoimmune disease, etc. This is why some researchers have concluded that BD is not just a psychiatric fault, but as a multi-system inflammatory disease.

When BD patients plunge into depression, there is an increase in C-reactive protein. This indicates that gut inflammation is connected to mood swings. Besides, patients with irritable bowel syndrome (IBS) have over twice the rate of BD compared to the general population.

Leaky gut has also been linked with BD as gut chemicals like lipopolysaccharide find its way out of the gut, causing inflammation and mood symptoms. BD patients also often have gut bacteria formulation that is similar to that of people with inflammatory bowel disease, leading to the reduction of neurotransmitters like GABA, noradrenaline, serotonin, dopamine, etc.

Here are foods that worsen BD:

The Western Diet: The bad fat, refined carb, sugar, with less vegetables found in the Western diet are dangerous to BD patients. Switching to the Mediterranean diet can be a lot healthier. However, it may be difficult for BD patients to change their diet. With enough support, they can be successful at this. Asides the Mediterranean diet, the ketogenic diet, which features high fat and low carb, is equally promising. Studies show that the ketogenic diet aids stable moods. However, beware that the keto diet comes with certain side effects that can last days or weeks or even more long-term effects.

Caffeine: Caffeine has been found to heighten mania in BD patients. When taken moderately, it can elevate mood. However, it poses a risk of dangerous mood elevation, when taken excessively.

Gluten: Patients with BD are likely to develop celiac disease or non-celiac gluten sensitivity. Going gluten-free may be helpful. Naidoo notes always asking her patients to go Gluten-free for a week to see what happens.

Alcohol: A 2006 study showed that alcohol use puts BD patients at risk for depression, and increases the risk of not adhering to their medication regimens. People who drank more have been said to be at more risk of BD symptoms and a slower recovery from it.

Grape fruit juice, tyramine, and other foods that may interfere with medication: Grape fruit juice can inhibit the enzyme system that metabolize certain enzymes in the liver. In the process, it increases the blood levels of medications like anti-anxiety medications, antidepressants, mood stabilizers, stimulants and antipsychotics. It may inhibit medication function, and increases blood pressure. Cheese, meat, marmite, soy sauce, concentrated yeast extract, etc., are some foods rich in tyramine. 6:34

The following are mood-stabilizing foods and supplements:

Omega-3s: A 2003 study showed that people who ate more sea foods (a major source of Omega-3) had lower BD. Another 2011 study showed that people who received omega-3 supplementation had similar results.

N-acetylcysteine (NAC): A 2018 study shows that people's mood improve when given a combination of aspirin and NAC. Other studies have shown that NAC alone was effective against depression. However, NAC isn't found in food sources, but in the body. It converts into cysteine, which is found in onions, egg yolks, garlics, oats, red peppers, yeast, and dairy products.

Folate and Folic Acid: Some studies have shown that these can help against depressive symptoms and prevent patients from relapsing. Leafy greens, bananas, legumes, cooked lentils and kidney beans, citrus fruits, meat, avocadoes, egg, almonds, etc. are food sources of folate and folic acid.

Magnesium: A 1999 study showed that magnesium help against BD symptoms without harmful side effect. Although, studies linking magnesium with BD aren't airtight, magnesium-rich foods can be just vital. Nuts, spinach, avocado, black beans, peanut butter are great sources of magnesium.

Zinc: A 2016 study linked BD with decreased zinc in people suffering from BD. Zinc-rich foods is thus important for BD sufferers, especially during the depressive phases of their illnesses. Sea foods, lean meant, egg yolks, and poultry (chicken and turkey) are sources of zinc.

Schizophrenia

People with schizophrenia have less diversity of bacteria, and with some unique bacteria not found in healthy guts. When this unique bacteria were transferred into healthy mice (in a study) the mice also showed symptoms of SCZ. This is peculiar to their brain chemistry.

SCZ patients have also been found to experience more gut problems such as inflammation, food intolerances, leaky gut, IBS, etc. than people who don't suffer from SCZ. Asides differences in gut bacteria, SCZ sufferers also experience differences in the bacteria of the mouth and throat. However, diet can play a key role in addressing this.

The following are foods that worsen Schizophrenia:

The Western Diet: A 2015 study showed that people who ate foods with a higher ration of unhealthy fats to total calories are more associate with SCZ. One reason for this is that SCZ patients have insufficient energy supply in the brain. As a result of which fats are broken down at an increased rate, thus posing some harm to the brain.

Gluten: In 1966, some researchers linked SCZ with weed consumption during the WW2. Most SCZ patients have been found to be prone to celiac disease and non-celiac sensitivity. Gluten-free meals are thus more preferable. Some foods to avoid include bread products, pasta, pizza, and cereals.

Sugar: Refined sugar is risky in SCZ patients. SCZ patients have been found to be more prone to diabetes than regular people. Some studies have also shown that the more SCZ patients took refined sugar, sweetened drinks, etc.

Alcohol: Several SCZ patients have been found to have a history of alcohol abuse. Studies have also shown that those who drank more than twenty drinks per week were more susceptible to SCZ symptoms. Very little to no drinks at all were found to be more helpful in people with SCZ

The following are foods that can help against SCZ:

Omega-3s: A 2009 study showed that Omega-3s helps to reduce positive and negative SCZ symptoms compared to placebo. Other recent studies have established.

N-acetylcysteine (NAC): SCZ patients have abnormal stress metabolism which causes oxidative stress. Also, the release of non-radicals also damage the brain tissues, thus sabotaging its defense systems. However, NAC has been found to raise chemicals that protect the brain and improves its defense system. This helps us see that NAC can be effective against SCZ.

Alpha-lipoic Acid: It is an anti-oxidant which protects the brain from excessive inflammation. Studies have shown that it can effectively address overall symptoms of SCZ and also improve cognition. It has also been found helpful against weight-gain and movement-abnormalities often caused by anti-psychotic medications. It can be found in vegetables, spinach, tomatoes and organ meats.

Vitamin C: Studies have confirmed that Vitamin C can be helpful against SCZ.

B Vitamins (folate): These aids metabolism and helps in the overall health of the brain. High B vitamin (particularly folate) have been linked to lower SCZ symptoms. Vegetables, low sugar cereals, fortified whole grains are high in folate. Meats and dairy products, vegetables, fortified whole grains, low-sugar cereals, are high in folate.

L-Theanine: This is a unique amino acid which enhances alpha brain waves, relaxation waves, and boosting brain-calming chemicals like GABA. It also reduces insomnia and SCZ symptoms in patients. It is found in tea products like green, black, and oolong teas. Yet, some moderation is required as they contain caffeine.

Melatonin: This is a sleep hormone (already discussed in chapter 8). It has been proven to be effective against insomnia in SCZ patients. Also, through its antioxidant and anti-inflammatory effects. Fish, eggs, nuts, tomatoes, oats, olives, grapes, etc. are some great sources.

Chapter 10: Libido: Oxytocin, Fenugreek, and the Science of Aphrodisiac

In this chapter, Naidoo examines Libido-related problems and how diet can be used to resolve them. Libido has been defined in various ways over time. However, the common thread is that libido is an instinctual drive similar to hunger. Like hunger, libido causes us to behave in certain ways; this is why you can prioritize them above anything else. They are controlled by the area of brain associated with pleasure. Hunger and libido also involve similar chemical – dopamine – which plays a huge role in both.

There are two male sex hormones – estrogen and testosterone. They are otherwise known as the female and male sex hormones. Still, both men and women share the two hormones, as they all have roles to play in their sexual health. Also, gut bacteria plays important roles in the regulation of these hormones. A 2014 study showed that gut bacteria influenced sexual function in mice, proving the same possibility in human.

The following are foods and substances that hamper libido:

The Western Diet: Studies have linked high fat and high calorie diets to poor testicular function, poor sperm production and potency since they lead to leaky gut, causing endotoxins to be released in the body. This causes low grade inflammation throughout the body, thus impairing sexual and reproductive performance for both men and female. Other studies have shown that high protein, low carb and fat diets improve sexual function.

Soy protein: A study has shown that soy consumption can disrupt libido reproduction. Many researchers believe that the estrogen released by soy-based products can cause men to develop breast and lose their sexual ability. However, this is generally inconclusive.

Alcohol: Some studies have shown that affects sexual function. A 2018 survey on men who depended on alcohol for their sex life: 37% of their subjects reported sexual dysfunction, 25%

reported ED, 20% reported unsatisfying orgasm, while 15.5% reported premature ejaculation, and a smaller percent of them reported excessive libido. It plays a key role in women's libido too – suppressing orgasm in young women. But moderate drinking shouldn't take a toll on one's sex life.

Sugar: Excessive sugar-beverage intake has been associated with lower testosterone levels. High sugar diet also leads to higher lepton levels, culminating in lower testosterone. Cutting down on sugar, sweetened drinks, sugar-rich snacks can improve sexual life.

Liquorice: It is a type of sweet that is harmful to libido. It has been associated to lower testosterone levels. It can be found in certain teas and chewing gums. Eating less candy of any sort helps reduce its consumption.

Perfluorooctanoic Acid (PFOA): PFOA is a chemical with multiple uses. It is most commonly used in making cookware and food packaging. Ingestion can lead to the disruption of the endocrine system, thus affecting sexual health. It has been proven to turn off androgen, thus reducing testosterone. It has also been said to be linked to infertility. Thankfully, manufacturers are beginning to use alternatives in their products.

The following are aphrodisiacs and libido-enhancing foods:

Oxytocin-boosting foods: Oxytocin is known as the "bonding hormone" due to its connection to sex, love and child rearing. It is also involved in libido and the heightening of arousal. It is the hormone released during orgasm for both men and women. It also plays a role in the registration and expression of emotions. Even though it cannot be gotten directly from food, there are foods that can help raise its levels. Dark chocolates, magnesium-rich diets like meat, green vegetables, nuts, seeds, unprocessed grains, eggs, etc. contain oxytocin.

Coffee: Caffeine intake has been linked with improved sexual function and satisfaction. However, excessive caffeine may pose a challenge.

Red wine: A 2009 study showed that moderate consumption of red wine has been found to enhance sexual function in women. It has also been linked to increased testosterone in men.

Pistachios and other nuts: A 2011 study on the sexual function of seventeen married men who were given 100g of pistachios for three weeks. Results showed that it aided with erection, a reduction in bad cholesterol and an increase in good cholesterol. It has also been found to also enhance arousal, lubrication, orgasm and satisfaction in women.

Saffron: Asides its anti-depressant functions, some studies have shown that saffron can increase libido and semen quality.

Fenugreek: Fenugreek is delicious but potent herb with a very powerful smell that takes long to wear out. It has been found to boost libido and increase testosterone in men, and sexual desire in both sexes. Its seeds can be crushed, boiled in water and consumed as a tea flavor. Even though its extracts are available as supplements, it is better taken from food.

Apples: A 2014 study on apples showed that regular apple intake aids lubrication and sexual function in women. They are rich in Vitamin C and Potassium. They also have antioxidant and anti-inflammatory properties.

Pomegranate juice: Studies have found them to enhance testosterone levels by 24%.It has been found to increase sperm levels. It can also serve as antioxidant. It is advised that you make your own juice from its seeds as commercial products may have extremely high sugar content.

Chili peppers: Capsaicin in chili peppers have been found to increase testosterone levels. A 2015 study showed that chili peppers increased testosterone levels.

Onions: It may have beneficial effects on testosterone. There are also indicators that it is good for libido.

Avocadoes: The Aztecs names avocado trees "testicle tree" in that it appears like the male testicle. They are sources of boron, an element that is vital for the production of sex hormones for both sexes.

Ayurvedic libido enhancers: Adding to readily-available food, a few traditional herbs and supplements have been thought to increase libido. The ayurvedic tradition stems from the Ayurveda, a health system which originated in India. Even though it is an ancient tradition, it has many practitioners today. It has numerous ways of addressing sexual dysfunction. If you are unsatisfied with western medicine, medication or diet on libido, you can learn more about the Ayurveda. To learn more, you can visit the *National Ayurvedic Medical Association* which represents the ayurvedic practice in the USA.

Background Information about *Your Brain on Food* by Uma Naidoo, MD.

Your Brain on Food by Uma Naidoo is a ten-chapter book written to address the role of food on the health of the brain and gut. The book provides a detailed information on the foods, supplements, and recipes that are either ideal or dangerous in addressing different mental cases. It is a diet book originally published in August 2020.

Cover Questions

- What is the connection between psychiatry and nutrition?
- How does gut imbalance affect the brain?
- Why are diets important to mental health?

Discussion Questions

- What chemicals are found in the brain
- Discuss the central nervous system (CNS) and the autonomic nervous system (ANS).
- How can poor food choices result in bad moods?
- What is the Mediterranean eating Pattern (MEP)?
- What are probiotics and prebiotics? What are their functions
- Why has modern psychiatry failed to see that the root of mental illnesses isn't always in the brain
- What kinds of bacteria are in the guts, and what are their functions?
- What are the substances can lead to the promotion of good moods?
- How can caffeine worsen anxiety?
- How does magnesium help to reduce anxiety?
- Discuss the causes of Dementia.
- Discuss Post-traumatic Stress Disorder (PTSD). What are its causes?
- Discuss the connection between libido and hunger.
- Where do the chemicals produced by the brain come from?
- What role does the connection of the gut and the brain play in dementia?
- What is Insomnia?
- What is a Bipolar Disorder? How does it cause fatigue?
- What foods help to address Bipolar Disorder?

Made in the USA
Columbia, SC
16 February 2021

33041853R00026